Patterns with Pandas

By Bobby Kennedy Shea

GS
MATH

Please visit our website, www.garethstevens.com. For a free color catalog of all our high-quality books, call toll free 1-800-542-2595 or fax 1-877-542-2596.

Library of Congress Cataloging-in-Publication Data

Shea, Bobby Kennedy.
Patterns with pandas / by Bobby Kennedy Shea.
   p. cm. – (Animal math)
Includes index.
ISBN 978-1-4339-9319-0 (pbk.)
ISBN 978-1-4339-9320-6 (6-pack)
ISBN 978-1-4339-9318-3 (library binding)
1. Pattern perception—Juvenile literature. 2. Giant panda—Juvenile literature. I. Title.
BF311.S25 2014
516.15—dc23

First Edition

Published in 2014 by
Gareth Stevens Publishing
111 East 14th Street, Suite 349
New York, NY 10003

Copyright © 2014 Gareth Stevens Publishing

Designer: Nicholas Domiano
Editor: Therese M. Shea

Photo credits: Cover, p. 1 Rich Carey/Shutterstock.com; pp. 3–24 (background texture) Natutik/Shutterstock.com; p. 5 Zoonar/Thinkstock.com; pp. 6, 8, 10, 16 iStockphoto/Thinkstock.com; pp. 7, 13, 17, 18 iStockphoto/Thinkstock.com; p. 9 stockpix4u/Shutterstock.com; p. 11 Hemera/Thinkstock.com; p. 14 falk/Shutterstock.com; pp. 15, 21 Comstock/Thinkstock.com; p. 19 © iStockphoto.com/mehmettorlak; p. 21 Katrina Brown/Shutterstock.com;

Printed in the United States of America

CPSIA compliance information: Batch #CS13GS: For further information contact Gareth Stevens, New York, New York at 1-800-542-2595.

Contents

Black-and-White Bear 4

Hungry Pandas! 8

Panda Cubs 10

Panda Pals 12

Panda Sounds 14

Panda Play 16

Pandas in Trouble 18

Red Pandas? 20

Glossary 22

Answer Key 22

For More Information 23

Index 24

Boldface words appear in the glossary.

Black-and-White Bear

Giant pandas are black and white. They can help us learn about **patterns**! Check your answers on page 22.

Look at the pattern. What color comes next?

Giant pandas have black fur around their eyes. They have black ears. Their fur keeps them warm.

Look at the pattern. What picture comes next?

  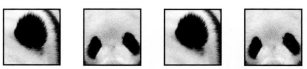 ?

Hungry Pandas!

Pandas are always eating! Pandas have strong teeth. They eat about 25 kinds of **bamboo**.

Numbers can make patterns, too. What number is missing?

22, 23, 24, ___?___

Panda Cubs

Panda babies are called cubs. They're very small at first. Their eyes are closed.

Which animal is missing in the pattern, a panda cub or a mother panda?

Panda Pals

Giant pandas live in the mountains of China. Some pandas live alone. Others live in small groups.

What number is missing in the pattern?

3 pandas, 5 pandas, __?__ pandas, 9 pandas

Panda Sounds

Pandas don't roar like other bears. They make sounds like goats! They honk, bark, and growl, too.

Read the sound pattern. What sound is missing?

Baa! Honk! Bark! Growl! Baa! Honk! __?__ Growl!

15

Panda Play

Pandas like to play. They climb on things. In zoos, they even play with toys!

Two balls are missing from the pattern. Which are missing?

    ? ?

Pandas in Trouble

There are not many giant pandas left. People are trying to help them.

Which groups are missing in the pattern?

 ? ?

Red Pandas?

Red pandas don't look like giant pandas. They're more like raccoons! The rings on a red panda's tail are a pattern, too!

Where else do you see patterns in our world?

Glossary

bamboo: a giant grass with long hollow stems that grows in warm, wet areas

pattern: the way colors, shapes, or numbers happen over and over again

Answer Key

page 4: black

page 6: picture of panda ear

page 8: 25

page 10: panda cub

page 12: 7

page 14: Bark!

page 16: blue ball, yellow ball

page 18: group of 3 pandas, group of 4 pandas

For More Information

Books

Gish, Melissa. *Pandas*. Mankato, MN: Creative Education, 2012.

Harris, Nancy. *Shapes and Patterns We Know*. Vero Beach, FL: Rourke Publishing, 2008.

Schreiber, Anne. *Pandas*. Washington, DC: National Geographic, 2010.

Websites

Mammals: Giant Panda
www.sandiegozoo.org/animalbytes/t-giant_panda.html
Check out this link to hear a giant panda.

Patterns
www.mathsisfun.com/algebra/patterns.html
Play games with patterns of colors, numbers, and shapes.

Publisher's note to educators and parents: Our editors have carefully reviewed these websites to ensure that they are suitable for students. Many websites change frequently, however, and we cannot guarantee that a site's future contents will continue to meet our high standards of quality and educational value. Be advised that students should be closely supervised whenever they access the Internet.

Index

bamboo 8

China 12

color 4

cubs 10

ears 6

eyes 6, 10

fur 6

mother panda 10

mountains 12

numbers 8, 12

play 16

red pandas 20

sounds 14

teeth 8

toys 16

zoos 16